THE LITTLE CORSET BOOK

A WORKBOOK ON PERIOD UNDERWEAR

Bonnie Holt Ambrose

Costume & Fashion Press
an imprint of
Quite Specific Media Group Ltd.
Hollywood

Email: info@quitespecificmedia.com

Voice: 323.851.5797
Fax: 323.851.5798

The Little Hatmaking Book and The Little Bodice Book were originally published by Drama Publishers.

Quite Specific Media Group Ltd. imprints include:

Drama Publishers
Costume & Fashion Press
EntertainmentPro
By Design Press
Jade Rabbit

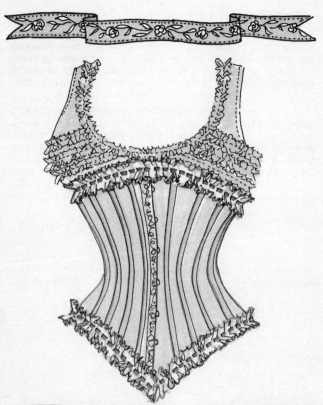

CORSET · · 1890

PATTERN MAKING...1890's CORSET

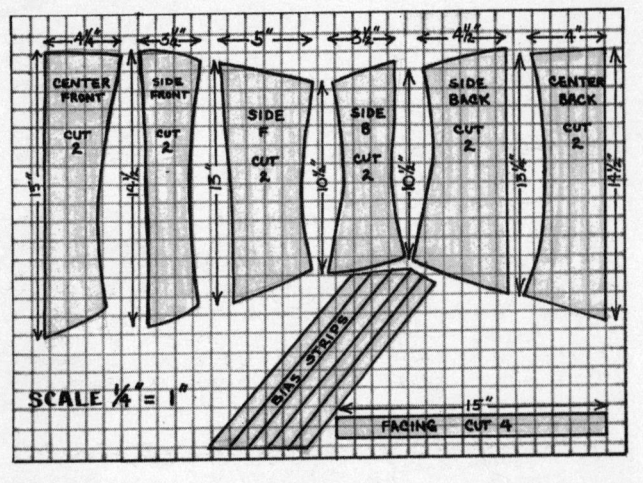

SCALE ¼" = 1"

FOLLOW THE GRID ABOVE AND TRANSFER THE PATTERN PIECES TO TRU-GRID PELLON OR 1" GRID PAPER. CAREFULLY FOLLOW MEASUREMENTS AND DRAW ALL DIRECTIONS ONTO THE PATTERN PIECES WITH A FELT PEN. IF A DIFFERENT SIZE CORSET IS DESIRED, SEE THE CHART ON PAGE ELEVEN.

CUT OUT PATTERN PIECES AND PIN TO COTTON CORSET FABRIC; THE IDEAL FABRIC IS COTTON COUTIL, A DRILL CLOTH, A SATIN BROCADE, OR CANVAS. THE CORSET WILL NOT BE LINED, THEREFORE TIGHTLY WOVEN COTTON FABRIC IS SUGGESTED.

PRE-SHRINK CANVAS AND DRILL CLOTH. PRESS.

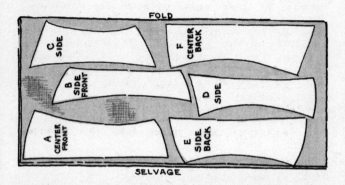

ARRANGE PATTERN PIECES CAREFULLY ON FOLDED FABRIC. PATTERN PIECES SHOULD BE PLACED WITH THE FABRIC GRAIN (AS SHOWN ABOVE). PIN AND CUT OUT. THE REMAINING FABRIC WILL BE USED TO CUT BIAS STRIPS TO FINISH TOP AND BOTTOM EDGE OF CORSET. USE A CHALK PENCIL AND IDENTIFY ALL CUT OUT PIECES ON THE WRONG SIDE OF THE FABRIC.

PIN CORSET PIECES TOGETHER WITH THE WRONG SIDES FACING. LEAVE THE CENTER FRONT AND CENTER BACK SEAMS OPEN. USING ½" SEAMS, MACHINE STITCH CORSET PIECES TOGETHER. THESE RAW SEAMS WILL BE FINISHED WITH RIBBON STAY COVERS. TRIM ALL SEAMS TO ¼" AND PRESS.

ADD A SATIN RIBBON WAIST BAND TO INSIDE OF CORSET TO REDUCE STRAIN ON THE FABRIC AT WAIST LINE.

PIN 1½" SATIN RIBBON IN POSITION AT EACH SEAM. AS RIBBON STAY COVERS ARE STITCHED IN PLACE THE RIBBON WAIST BAND WILL BE STITCHED ALSO.

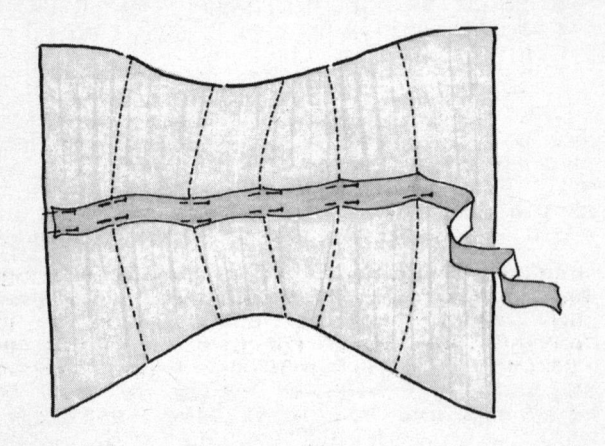

CHOOSE A COMPLEMENTARY COLOR FOR THE RIBBON STAY COVERS AS THIS WILL ACCENTUATE THE WAIST LINE AND SHAPE OF THE CORSET. THE RIBBON WIDTH IS IMPORTANT AS IT MUST COVER THE METAL STAY AND ALLOW FOR MACHINE STITCHING ON BOTH SIDES (AS SHOWN

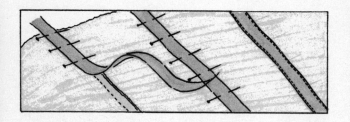

PLACE RIBBON OVER SEAM, PIN, AND SEW DOWN ONE SIDE AS CLOSE TO EDGE OF RIBBON AS POSSIBLE. SEW THE OTHER EDGE. CONTINUE THIS PROCEDURE UNTIL ALL SEAMS ARE COVERED. USE A CHALK PENCIL TO MARK WHERE THE REMAINING STAY COVERS WILL BE SEWN. PIN RIBBON STAY COVERS IN POSITION AND MACHINE STITCH.

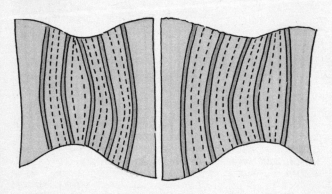

ON THE GOOD SIDE OF FABRIC PIN FRONT FACING
TO CENTER FRONT RIGHT SIDE.   LAY CLASP 1"
DOWN FROM TOP OF CORSET. USE PENCIL TO
MARK BOTH SIDES OF EACH CLASP. PIN AT EACH
MARK.   MACHINE STITCH BETWEEN STRAIGHT
PINS.   BACKSTITCH AT EACH STOPPING POINT.
PRESS OPEN SEAM.

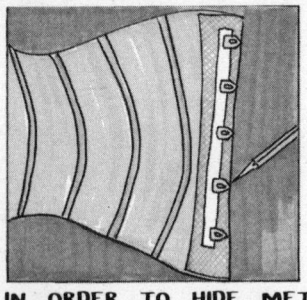 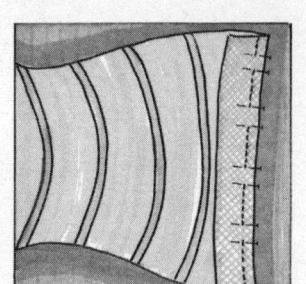

IN ORDER TO HIDE METAL CLASPS A BROCADE
RIBBON CAN BE ADDED.   STITCH RIBBON DOWN
FRONT OF PRESSED OPEN SEAM AS SHOWN.

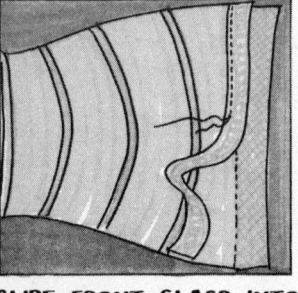 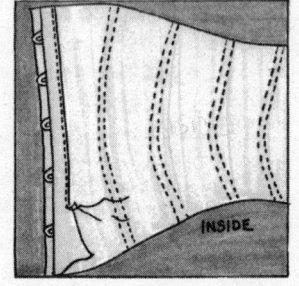

SLIDE FRONT CLASP INTO OPENINGS.   USE ZIPPER
FOOT TO STITCH THROUGH ALL FABRIC LAYERS
NEXT TO CLASP.

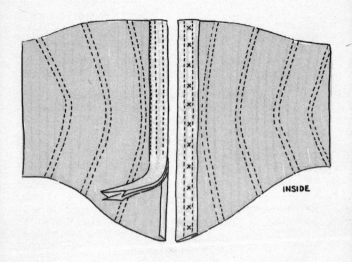

INSIDE

PIN 2 ½" WIDE FACING AND INTERFACING TO
OUTER FABRIC AT BACK OPENING, MACHINE
STITCH ½" SEAM, PRESS AND FOLD TO INSIDE OF
CORSET BACK. PRESS AND PIN IN POSITION.
SEW FIRST ROW OF STITCHES ½" IN FROM
OUTSIDE EDGE. LEAVE ½" SPACE FOR EYELETS
AND STITCH A SECOND SEAM. SEW A FINAL ROW
OF STITCHES AT OUTER EDGE OF FACING. THE
FINISHED BACK CORSET SHOULD HAVE A CENTER
AISLE FOR EYELETS ENCLOSED BY BONING ON
EITHER SIDE.

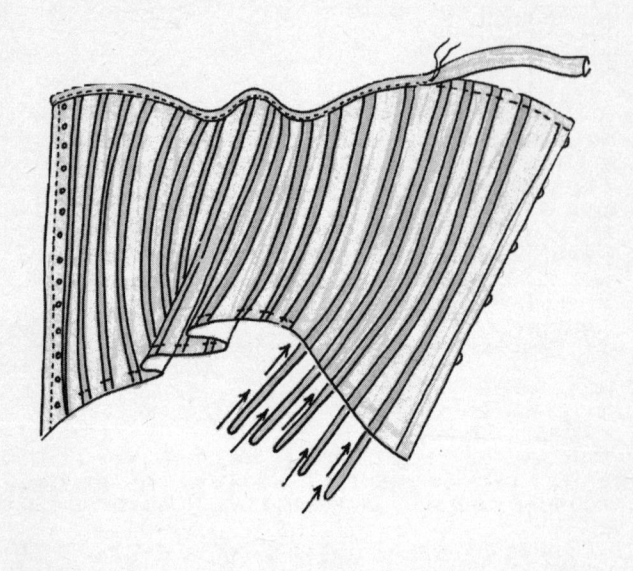

FINISH THE TOP EDGE OF THE CORSET WITH BIAS
TAPE IN THE SAME FABRIC.   MACHINE STITCH
BIAS TAPE TO TOP OUTSIDE EDGE OF CORSET.
FOLD BIAS TAPE TO INSIDE AND MACHINE STITCH
DOWN.   SLIDE THE APPROPRIATE LENGTH METAL
STAYS INTO THE RIBBON CASINGS.   TACK STITCH
3/4" FROM BOTTOM EDGE OF CORSET.

FINISH THE BOTTOM EDGE OF CORSET WITH BIAS
TAPE JUST AS THE TOP EDGE WAS COMPLETED.

LAY CORSET FLAT WITH BACK OPENING EVEN AND
MARK WHERE ALL EYELETS WILL BE INSERTED.

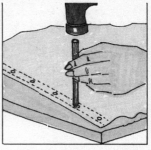

USE A SMALL EYELET HOLE PUNCH TO CUT
THROUGH ALL LAYERS. WORK ON TOP OF A
DISPOSABLE PIECE OF WOOD. PRACTICE SETTING
THE EYELETS FIRST BY USING SCRAP FABRIC.
YOU WILL NEED A SMALL HAMMER AND A METAL
EYELET SETTER. INSERT EYELETS FROM TOP
SIDE OF FABRIC. FLIP CORSET OVER AND SET
EYELETS FROM INSIDE. EYELETS SHOULD SPREAD
AND CLAMP INTO FABRIC TIGHTLY.

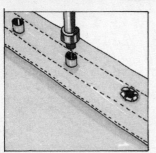
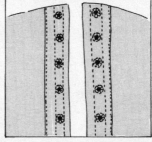

USING AN 8 YARD LACE, START LACING CORSET AT TOP AS SHOWN. PULL EXTRA LACE LENGTH OUT AT WAIST AREA.
CONTINUE TO LACE TO BOTTOM OF CORSET. TIE BOW AND KNOT. USE WAIST LACES FOR ADJUSTMENTS. WRAP LACES AROUND WAIST ONCE THEN TIE IN BOW AT BACK.

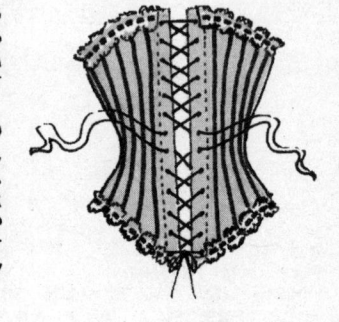

FABRIC AND NOTIONS: (SIZE 12) 1 YD. FABRIC, 2½ YDS. ¼" SATIN RIBBON, 2½ YDS. INSERTION LACE, 1 YD. 1" BROCADE RIBBON, ½ YD. IRON-ON CANVAS INTERFACING, 12" METAL CENTER FRONT CLASP, 30 #2 METAL EYELETS, EYELET SETTER, HOLE PUNCH, 8 YD. SHOE LACE.

¼" METAL STAYS : 6/ 12", 10/ 11", 4/ 10", 12/ 9", 2/ 8".

SIZE CONVERSION CHART

SIZE	6	8	10	12	14	16	18	20
BUST	34	35	36	38	40	42	44	46
WAIST	25	26	27	28	31	34	38	40
HIP	35	36	37	39	42	44	48	50
BACK	15¾	16	16¼	16½	16½	16¾	17	17½

METAL STAYS ─────────────────

SIZE 6 - 6/11", 10/10", 4/9", 8/8", 2/7"
SIZE 8 - 6/12", 10/11", 4/10", 10/9", 2/8"
SIZE 10 - 6/12", 10/11", 4/10", 12/9", 2/8"
SIZE 12 - 6/12", 10/11", 4/10", 12/9", 2/8"
SIZE 14 - 6/12", 10/11", 4/10", 14/9", 2/8"
SIZE 16 - 6/13", 10/12", 4/11", 16/10", 2/9"
SIZE 18 - 6/13", 10/12", 4/11", 18/10", 2/9"
SIZE 20 - 6/14", 10/13", 4/12" 20/11", 2/10"

THESE QUANTITIES FOR METAL STAYS ARE APPROXIMATE AND MAY CHANGE AS THE CORSET IS FITTED AND TAKEN UP.

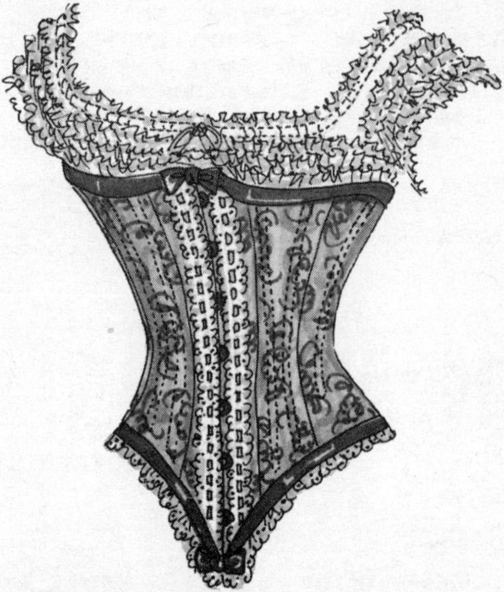

CORSET···1860

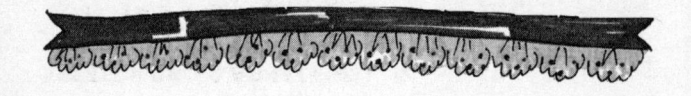

PATTERN MAKING ··· 1860'S CORSET

CUT TWO EACH OF THE PATTERN PIECES, PLUS
TWO EACH FOR THE CORSET LINING.

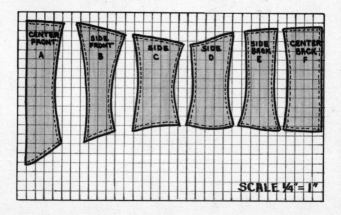

CENTER FRONT A — SIDE FRONT B — SIDE C — SIDE D — SIDE BACK E — CENTER BACK F

SCALE ¼" = 1"

TO ENLARGE AN EXISTING CORSET PATTERN TAKE
CAREFUL MEASUREMENTS OF THE SUBJECT AND
COMPARE THE MEASUREMENTS TO THE PATTERN
PIECES. REMEMBER THAT THERE ARE 24 SEAM
EDGES IN A 12 PIECE CORSET. IF YOU NEED AN
EXTRA 3" IN THE UNDER-BUST AREA, THEN
DIVIDE 3" BY 24. YOU WILL BE ADDING ⅛" TO
EACH SEAM. IF 6" IS NEEDED IN THE HIP AREA,
THEN DIVIDE 6" BY 24 AND ADD ¼" TO EACH
SEAM EDGE.

SIZE ENLARGEMENT DIAGRAM

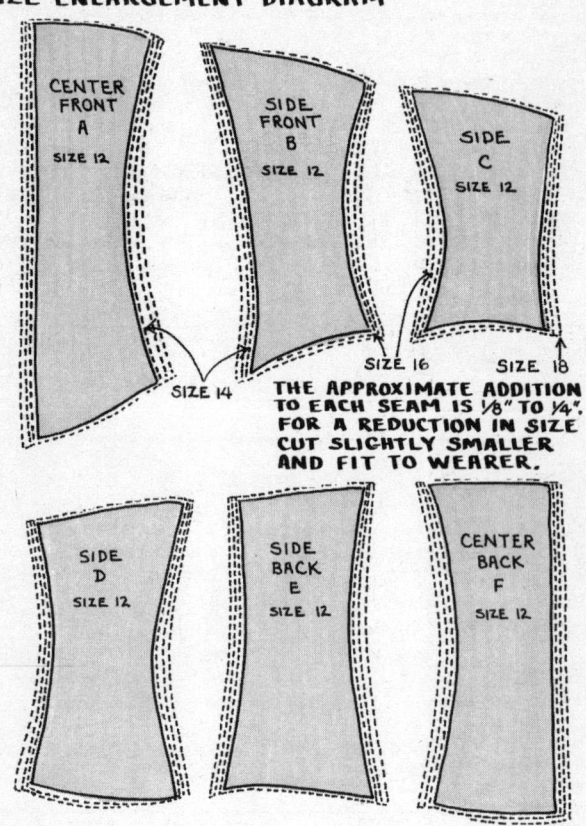

CENTER FRONT A
SIZE 12

SIDE FRONT B
SIZE 12

SIDE C
SIZE 12

SIZE 14

SIZE 16   SIZE 18

THE APPROXIMATE ADDITION TO EACH SEAM IS ⅛" TO ¼". FOR A REDUCTION IN SIZE CUT SLIGHTLY SMALLER AND FIT TO WEARER.

SIDE D
SIZE 12

SIDE BACK E
SIZE 12

CENTER BACK F
SIZE 12

CUT TWO LAYERS OF OUTER FABRIC AND TWO
LAYERS OF LINING FABRIC FOR PATTERN PIECES
"A" THRU "F". PIN SEAMS TOGETHER AS
INDICATED IN ILLUSTRATION AND MACHINE STITCH.

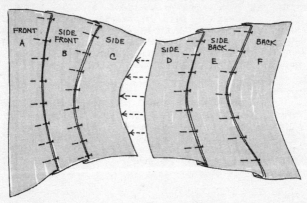

THE BEST FIT WILL COME FROM BASTING THE
LINING TOGETHER FOR A FIRST FITTING. CUT
THE LINING A LITTLE LARGER THAN YOU THINK
YOU NEED. USE THE LONGEST STITCH ON THE
SEWING MACHINE AND SEW ALL SEAMS
TOGETHER INCLUDING THE FRONT CLOSURE.

REMEMBER THAT REDUCTION OF THE WAISTLINE
IS THE MAIN PURPOSE OF THE CORSET AND TAKE
UP ACCORDINGLY.

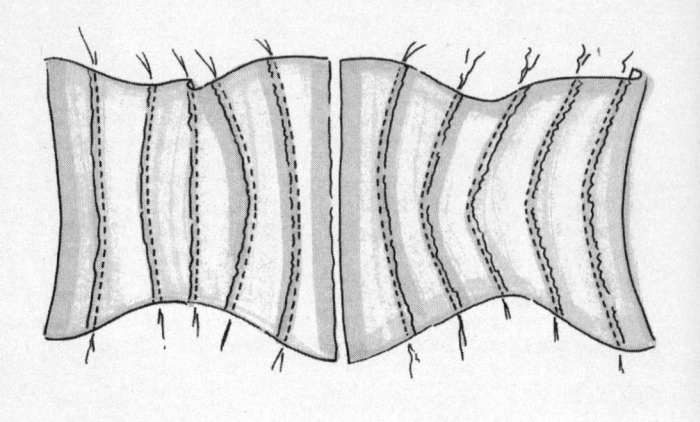

FIT CORSET NOW. PIN OR BASTE THE CENTER FRONT SEAM. THE BACK SEAM OF THE CORSET SHOULD HAVE A GAP OF UP TO 2". THE CORSET SHOULD LOOK SMOOTH ON THE BODY. ADJUSTMENTS CAN BE EASILY MADE BY TAKING UP SEAMS IN LARGER CORSET SECTIONS.

AFTER ALL SEAMS HAVE BEEN TAKEN UP TO THE CORRECT SIZE AND MACHINED STITCHED, TRIM EACH SEAM TO THE REQUIRED ¼" SIZE. STEAM PRESS EACH SEAM IN THE SAME DIRECTION ACROSS THE WIDTH OF THE CORSET. TURN CORSET OVER AND PRESS AGAIN. YOU ARE NOW READY TO APPLY THE RIBBON STAY COVERS.

HAVE A FRIEND HELP WITH THIS FITTING. THERE
SHOULD BE A 2" GAP AT BACK OPENING FOR
REDUCTION OF THE WAIST. START TAKING UP
SEAMS A LITTLE AT A TIME UNTIL THE CORRECT
FIT IS ACHIEVED. BE SURE TO TAKE THE SAME
AMOUNT OUT OF THE MATCHING SEAM ON THE
OTHER SIDE OF CORSET.

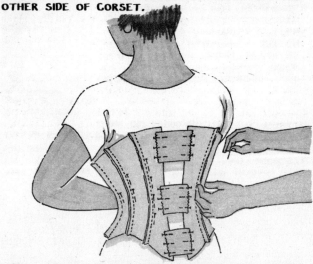

WHEN FITTING IS COMPLETE ON BOTH THE OUTER
FABRIC AND LINING, TRIM ALL SEAMS DOWN TO 1/4".

STEAM PRESS ALL SEAMS TOWARD BACK
OPENING. ON THE FRONT SIDE OF CORSET
REINFORCE SEAMS BY TOP STITCHING. FOLLOW
THE SAME PROCEDURE WITH CORSET LINING.

PIN CORSET OUTER FABRIC TO CORSET LINING.
LAY FRONT CLASP ON CORSET FRONT OPENING

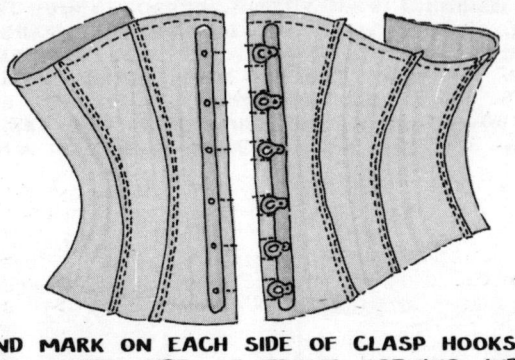

AND MARK ON EACH SIDE OF CLASP HOOKS. ON
THE OTHER SIDE OF FRONT OPENING INDICATE
WHERE HOLES WILL BE CUT FOR INSERTION OF
CLASP EYES. AT BACK OPENING STEAM PRESS IN
IRON-ON CANVAS TO STRENGTHEN
EYELET AREA.

MACHINE STITCH ACROSS TOP
OF CORSET AND DOWN BACK
SEAM. STITCH FRONT SEAM AS
INDICATED IN DRAWING. STITCH
UP TO MARKS AND BACK STITCH
TO LOCK THREAD. SKIP TO
NEXT MARK AND DO THE SAME.
THE METAL HOOKS OF THE
FRONT CLASP SHOULD SLIDE
EASILY INTO THESE OPENINGS.
TURN CORSET RIGHT SIDE OUT
AND STEAM PRESS.

SLIDE FRONT CLASP HOOKS INTO DESIGNATED
OPENINGS AND PIN IN POSITION. CHECK MARKS

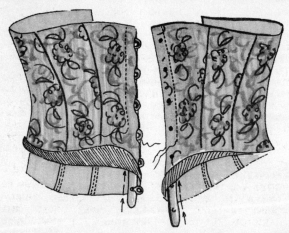

FOR HOLES ON THE OTHER SIDE OF FRONT
OPENING. USE AN ICE PICK OR NAIL TO PUNCH
SMALL HOLES FOR CLASP EYES. INSERT CLASP
EYES ONTO HOLES AND PIN CLASP FIRMLY
AGAINST SEAM. USE A ZIPPER FOOT TO STITCH
NEXT TO BOTH CLASP PIECES.

WITH A CHALK PENCIL MARK ON THE LINING
WHERE ALL STAYS WILL BE INSERTED. DRAW A
LINE ON EITHER SIDE OF THE STAY WHERE
STITCHING WILL BE LOCATED. MACHINE STITCH
AROUND EACH STAY POCKET LEAVING EACH
POCKET BOTTOM OPEN. SLIDE METAL STAYS
INTO EACH POCKET AND STITCH IT CLOSED AT
BOTTOM.

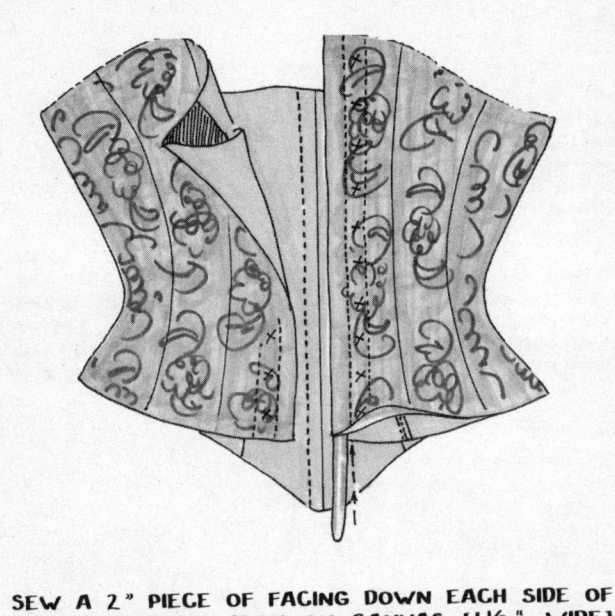

SEW A 2" PIECE OF FACING DOWN EACH SIDE OF
BACK OPENING. IRON-ON CANVAS [1½" WIDE]
SHOULD ALREADY BE APPLIED DOWN THE BACK
OPENING FOR EXTRA STRENGTH. TURN FACING
UNDER, STEAM PRESS, PIN AND MACHINE STITCH.
SEW A SEAM ⅜" FROM BACK EDGE TO CREATE
THE POCKET FOR A METAL STAY. INSERT
METAL STAYS IN POCKETS ON BOTH SIDES OF
BACK OPENING.

SPACE EYELETS 1¼" APART AND MARK WHERE THEY WILL BE INSERTED. USE A HAMMER AND SMALL HOLE PUNCH TO CUT THROUGH ALL LAYERS. WORK ON A PIECE OF WOOD. PUSH EYELETS THROUGH FROM FRONT SIDE OF FABRIC. FLIP FABRIC OVER AND SET EYELETS WITH METAL SETTING TOOL AND HAMMER.

TURN A ½" SEAM TO THE INSIDE ALONG CORSET BOTTOM EDGE. PRESS, PIN, AND STITCH CLOSED. PIN LACE AND RIBBON TRIM ALONG LOWER EDGE OF CORSET AND STITCH IN POSITION.

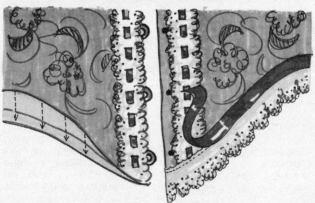

PIN LACE AND RIBBON TRIM TO TOP EDGE OF CORSET. HAND STITCH IN POSITION. FOR EXTRA TRIM, ADD A SMALL BOW AT TOP CENTER AND BOTTOM OF FRONT CLOSURE.

FABRIC AND NOTIONS: (SIZE 12) 1 YD. FABRIC, 1
1 YD. LINING FABRIC, 2½ YDS. 1" SATIN RIBBON,
1½ YDS. INSERTION LACE, 1½ YDS. INSERTION
RIBBON, 1 YDS. 1" EYELET LACE, ½ YD. IRON-
ON CANVAS INTERFACING, 14" METAL CENTER
FRONT CLASP, 30 #2 METAL EYELETS, EYELET
SETTER, HOLE PUNCH, 8 YD. SHOE LACE.

SUGGESTED FABRICS: SATIN BROCADE, SILK,
COTTON BROCADE, TAFFETA, COUTIL, SATIN
RIBBON, MOIRE TAFFETA RIBBON, VELVET RIBBON,
EYELET LACE, ANTIQUE LACE, CANVAS LINING,
BRUSHED COTTON LINING.

CHEMISE

PATTERN GRID

USE TRU-GRID AND DUPLICATE THE PATTERN BELOW. MAKE YOUR SIZE ADJUSTMENTS NOW. THE BUST AREA SHOULD MEASURE 2 TO 4"

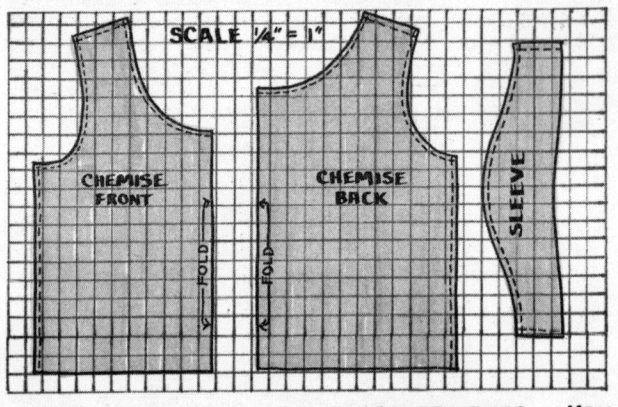

LARGER THAN YOUR OWN MEASUREMENTS. YOU CAN LENGTHEN OR SHORTEN THE CHEMISE AS DESIRED.

LAY THE TRU-GRID PATTERN PIECES ON YOUR FOLDED FABRIC. PLACE CHEMISE CENTER FRONT AND CENTER BACK ON THE FOLD. CUT OUT ALL THREE PIECES AND SOME 1½" BIAS TAPE STRIPS. SERGE TOGETHER SHOULDER SEAMS. GATHER TOP OF SLEEVE AND PIN INTO ARM EYE. SERGE IN PLACE. SERGE SLEEVE AND SIDE SEAM. ADD BIAS TAPE TO NECKLINE STARTING AT FRONT BELOW CENTER NECK. FINISH BIAS BY LEAVING

AN OPENING AT CENTER FRONT NECKLINE TO INSERT DRAWSTRING.

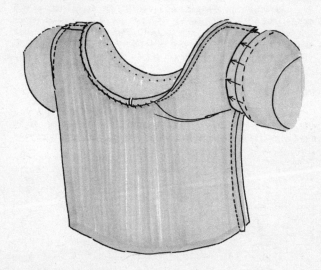

USE A SOFT BATISTE FABRIC FOR THE CHEMISE. CUT IT LARGER SO THAT IT CAN BE DRAWN UP AROUND THE NECKLINE. THE CHEMISE CAN BE SLEEVELESS, HAVE A NARROW SHOULDER, HAVE AMPLE LACE TRIM OR MADE PLAIN. THE CHEMISE MAKES THE CORSET A LITTLE MORE COMFORTABLE.

BEFORE SEWING SIDE SEAMS APPLY LACE TRIM.

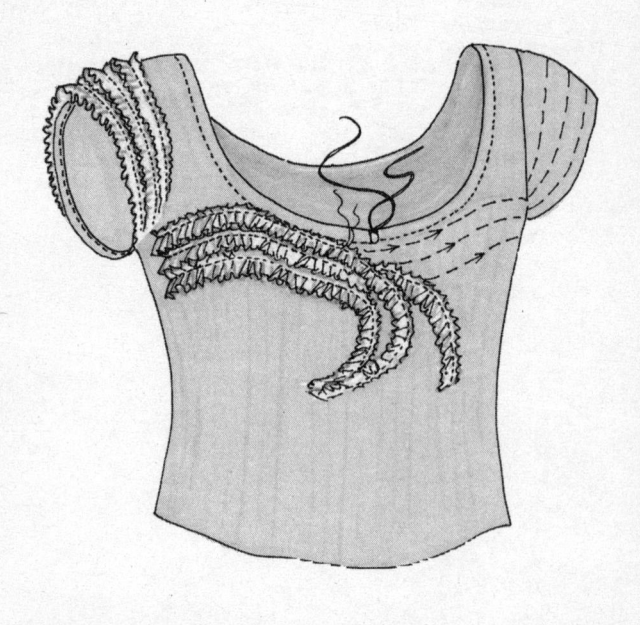

CHOOSE A SOFT OLD FASHIONED LACE FOR
CHEMISE TRIM. GATHER ALONG ONE EDGE AND
PIN TO CHEMISE AS DESIRED. DO NOT RUN LACE
INTO AREA WHERE CORSET WILL FIT. MACHINE
STITCH LACE TRIM TO CHEMISE. TINY RIBBON
TRIM IS A NICE COMPLEMENT.

ANTIQUE, HAND CROCHETED LACE CAN ADD A
SPECIAL TOUCH TO THESE BATISTE OR SILK TOPS.

TINY PEARL BUTTONS CAN BE
ADDED TO THE FRONT PLACKET.

FABRIC AND NOTIONS;
1½ YDS. BATISTE, 1-4
YDS. LACE, 42"
DRAWSTRING, 1 YD.
RIBBON.

SUGGESTED FABRICS:
BATISTE, SILK,
CHARMEUSE, SATIN
CORD, ANTIQUE LACE,
AND BUTTONS.

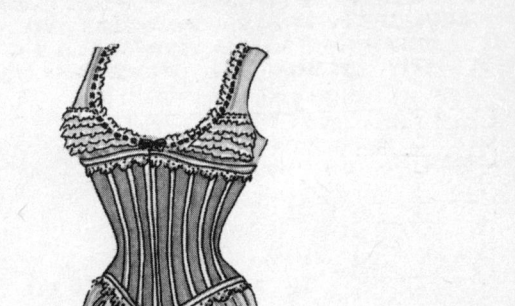

DRAWERS

DRAWERS

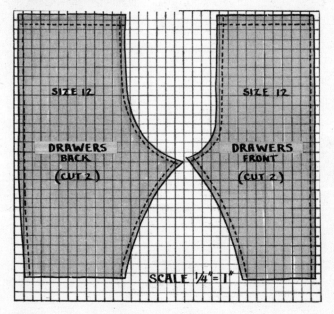

Within the illustration:

SIZE 12

SIZE 12

DRAWERS BACK (CUT 2)

DRAWERS FRONT (CUT 2)

SCALE 1/4"=1"

COPY THE DIMENSIONS FOR THESE SIZE 12 DRAWERS ONTO TRU-GRID FABRIC. ENLARGE BY ADDING THE EXTRA INCHES YOU NEED, EVENLY TO THE SIDE SEAMS. TRANSFER PATTERN TO FABRIC YOU HAVE CHOSEN. CUT OUT TWO FRONTS AND TWO BACKS.

SEW CENTER FRONT SEAMS TOGETHER. SEW CENTER BACK SEAMS TOGETHER. PIN FRONT TO BACK DRAWERS AND STITCH SIDE SEAMS TOGETHER. PRESS ALL SEAMS OPEN. LNSEAM WILL BE LEFT OPEN FOR EASY APPLICATION OF TRIM. FOLD 1" DOWN AT WAISTLINE FOR ELASTIC CASING. MACHINE STITCH CASING AND THREAD ELASTIC THROUGH. TIGHTEN AND TACK ELASTIC.

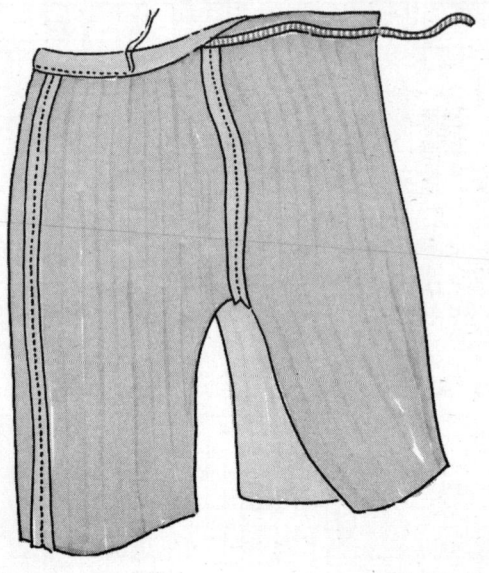

PIN ROWS OF EYELET OR LACE TRIM TO
DRAWERS LEGS. SEW ALL TRIM IN POSITION.
SEW INSEAM CLOSED.

FABRIC AND NOTIONS: 1½ YDS. FABRIC, 1½ YDS.
3" EYELET LACE, 3 YDS. 2" EYELET LACE,
1½ YDS. EYELET INSERTION LACE, 2 YDS.
INSERTION RIBBON. 1 YD. ½" ELASTIC.

TRIM DESIGNS CAN BE AS ORNATE AS DESIRED.
A FEW EXAMPLES ARE SHOWN.

CORSET···1750

CORSET · · · · 1750

FOLLOW THE GRID BELOW AND TRANSFER THE
PATTERN PIECES TO TRU-GRID PELLON OR 1" GRID
PAPER. CAREFULLY FOLLOW MEASUREMENTS AND
DRAW ALL DIRECTIONS ONTO THE PATTERN PIECES
WITH A FELT PEN. IF A DIFFERENT SIZE CORSET
IS DESIRED, SEE THE CHART AT THE BACK OF
THIS BOOK.

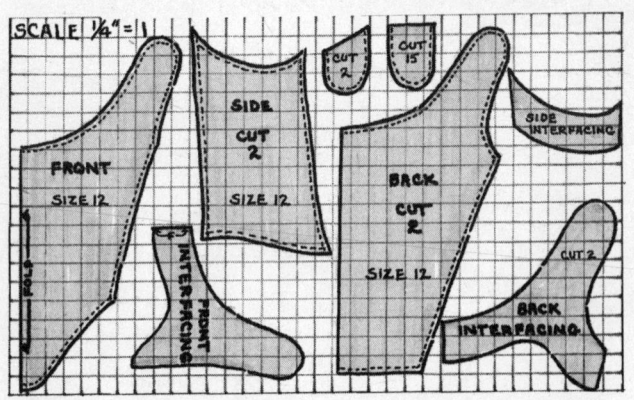

CUT OUT TRU-GRID PATTERN PIECES. ARRANGE
FRONT SIDE AND BACK PATTERN PIECES ON
FOLDED FABRIC. PIN IN POSITION AND CUT OUT.
CUT PEPLUM PIECES FROM REMAINING FABRIC.
CUT MATCHING LININGS FOR ALL OF THESE
PIECES. CUT SIDE, FRONT, AND BACK
INTERFACINGS FROM IRON-ON CANVAS.

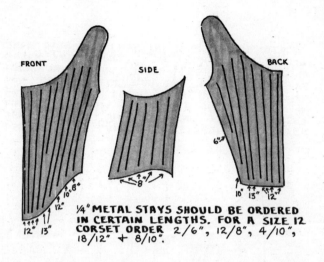

¼" METAL STAYS SHOULD BE ORDERED IN CERTAIN LENGTHS. FOR A SIZE 12 CORSET ORDER 2/6", 12/8", 4/10", 18/12" + 8/10".

THESE QUANTITIES FOR METAL STAYS ARE APPROXIMATE AND MAY CHANGE AS THE CORSET IS FITTED AND TAKEN UP.

AN INEXPENSIVE PRODUCT THAT WORKS WELL AS BONING IS METAL STRAPPING USED ON CRATES AND IN SHIPPING. THIS PRODUCT MUST HAVE THE ENDS TIPPED WITH A PLASTIC SEALER SO IT WILL NOT CUT THROUGH THE FABRIC. SPRAY PAINTING THIS METAL STRAPPING WITH A NON-RUSTING PAINT IS SUGGESTED. THE ADVANTAGE OF THIS METAL BONING IS COST AND THE ABILITY TO CUT IT TO THE EXACT SIZE.

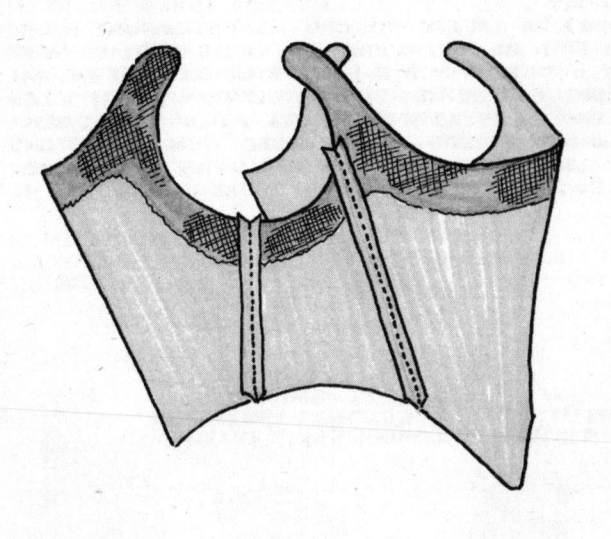

USE IRON-ON CANVAS INTERFACING TO STIFFEN
THE ARMHOLES AND NECKLINE OF THE CORSET
LINING.   STEAM PRESS ALL INTERFACINGS IN
POSITION.   SEW LINING FRONT BODICE SEAM TO
SIDE BODICE PIECE AND SIDE BODICE SEAM TO
LINING BACK BODICE PIECE [AS SHOWN].   SEW
OUTER FABRIC PIECES TO EACH OTHER IN THE
SAME MANNER. LEAVE THE BACK SEAMS OPEN.

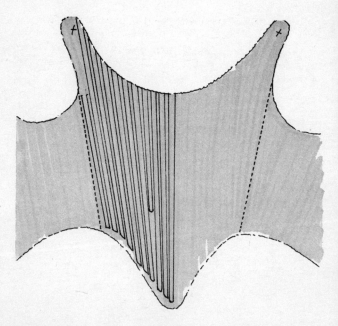

WITH PENCIL AND RULER DRAW STITCHING LINES
FOR EVERY STAY POCKET ON LINING FABRIC.
WORK ON THE TOPSIDE OF CORSET LINING
FABRIC. PIN OUTER CORSET TO CORSET LINING.
WITH LINING FACING UP MACHINE STITCH EACH
PENCIL LINE TO PRODUCE POCKETS FOR STAYS.
LEAVE TOP OF STAY POCKETS OPEN FOR
INSERTION OF STAYS. FINISH BOTTOM OF EACH
STAY POCKET BY MACHINE STITCHING 3/4" ABOVE
LOWER CORSET EDGE.

CUT ALL PEPLUM PIECES.
PIN AND MACHINE STITCH
EACH PIECE OF PEPLUM TO
LINING. TURN AND PRESS.
NUMBER OF PEPLUM TABS
WILL BE GOVERNED BY
WAIST LENGTH.

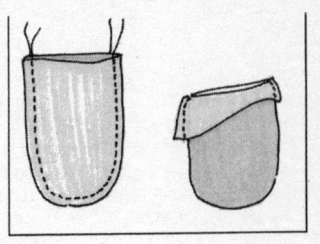

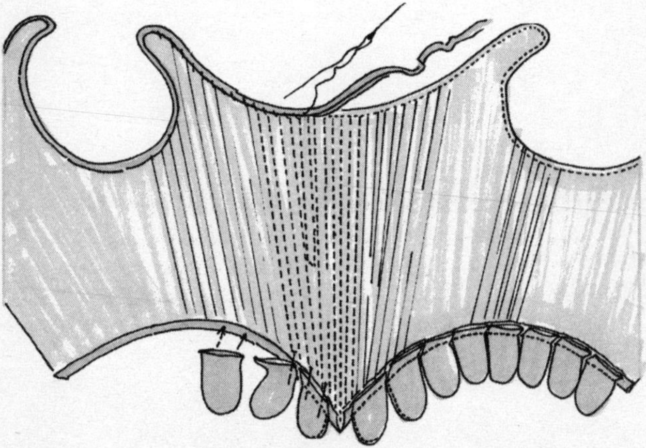

CAREFULLY PIN TAB PIECES TO WAIST SEAM OF
CORSET. VISUALLY CHECK TO BE SURE PEPLUM
TABS HANG CORRECTLY WHEN VIEWED FROM THE
FRONT. MACHINE STITCH PEPLUM TABS TO
CORSET WAIST. FINISH THE WAIST SEAM BY
SERGING OR COVER THE SEAM WITH BIAS TAPE.

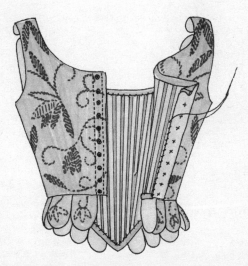

FINISH THE BACK OPENING OF THE CORSET IN A
SIMILAR MANNER AS THE VICTORIAN CORSET.
SEW A BACK FACING DOWN BOTH SIDES OF BACK
OPENING.   FOLD IN, PRESS, AND WHIP STITCH
FACING TO FINISH BACK SEAMS.   MARK WHERE
EYELETS (SMALL GROMMETS)   WILL BE
PLACED.   EYELETS SHOULD BE PLACED IN AISLE
BETWEEN TWO BACK PIECES OF BONING.   FOLLOW
DIRECTIONS FOR SETTING EYELETS ON PRECEDING
PAGES.   USE A 54" SHOE LACE TO FASTEN
CORSET.

FABRIC AND NOTIONS : I YD. FABRIC, I YD. LINING,
I ½ YDS. RIBBON, I YD. IRON-ON CANVAS, 20 SMALL
GROMMETS, HOLE PUNCH, GROMMET SETTER,
54" SHOE LACE.

METAL STAYS : (SIZE 12) 2/6", 12/8", 4/10",
                18/12", 8/10.

THESE QUANTITIES FOR METAL STAYS ARE
APPROXIMATE AND MAY CHANGE AS THE CORSET
IS FITTED AND TAKEN UP.

SUGGESTED FABRICS : EMBROIDERIED CREWEL,
TAPESTRY WEAVE, HEAVY BROCADE, WOOL,
VELVET, SATIN. LINING FABRIC- MUSLIN,
CANVAS, SATIN, COTTON.

CORSELET · · · 1700

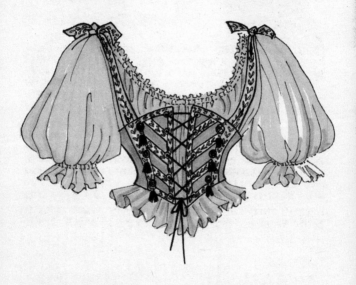

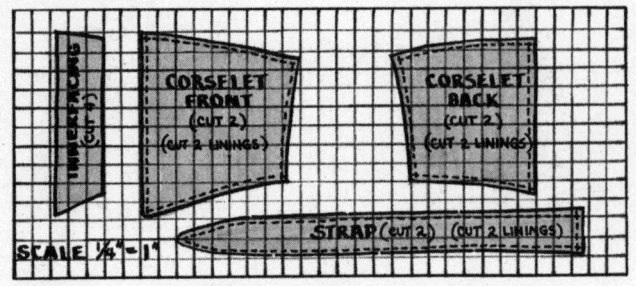

SCALE ¼" = 1"

FOLLOW THE GRID ABOVE AND TRANSFER THE
PATTERN PIECES TO TRU-GRID PELLON OR 1" GRID
PAPER. CAREFULLY FOLLOW MEASUREMENTS AND
DRAW ALL DIRECTIONS ONTO THE PATTERN
PIECES WITH A FELT PEN. IF A DIFFERENT SIZE
CORSET IS DESIRED, SEE THE CHART AT THE
BACK OF THIS BOOK.

CUT TWO EACH OF THE CORSELET FRONT, BACK
AND STRAPS. DO THE SAME WITH THE LINING
FABRIC. USE IRON-ON CANVAS TO CUT FOUR
FRONT INTERFACINGS. WITH THE RIGHT SIDES OF
FABRIC TOGETHER SEW THE BACK SEAM. SEW
SIDE SEAMS. PUT THE LINING PIECES TOGETHER
IN THE SAME WAY.

PRESS CANVAS INTERFACING TO LINING AT CENTER FRONT OPENING.

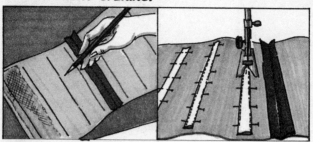

BONING WILL BE APPLIED ONLY TO CORSET LINING. USE A CHALK PENCIL TO INDICATE WHERE BONING WILL BE SEWN TO LINING. FEATHER WEIGHT BONING MAY BE USED INSTEAD OF METAL BONING. CUT BONING TO SIZE AND STEAM PRESS FLAT. PIN IN POSITION LEAVING A 3/4" SEAM AT THE TOP AND BOTTOM OF CORSELET. USE MACHINE TO STITCH DIRECTLY DOWN CENTER OF EACH PIECE OF BONING. AFTER ALL BONING IS APPLIED, STEAM PRESS CORSET LINING.

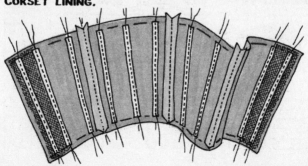

DECIDE BEFOREHAND WHAT LOOK YOU WANT TO
ACHIEVE WITH CHOICE OF FABRIC,
COLOR, TEXTURE, AND TRIM.

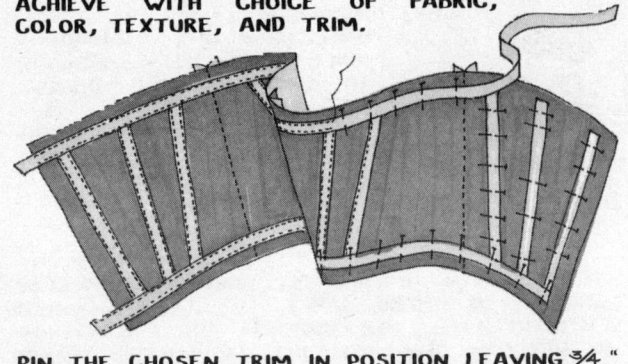

PIN THE CHOSEN TRIM IN POSITION LEAVING ¾"
SEAM ALLOWANCE ON OUTSIDE EDGES. MACHINE
STITCH ALL TRIM IN POSITION. PIN RIGHT SIDES
OF CORSELET TOGETHER AND SEW TOP, BOTTOM
AND ONE FRONT SEAM. LEAVE THE OTHER SEAM
OPEN FOR TURNING THE GARMENT. TURN RIGHT
SIDE OUT AND PRESS.

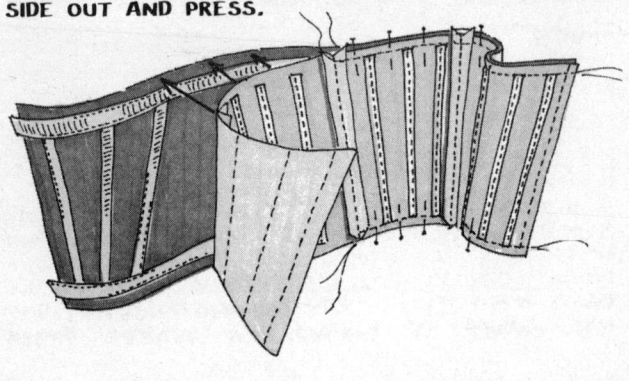

AFTER SEWING FRONT CORSET TO LINING, TURN
AND PRESS ON WRONG SIDE.   FOLD OPEN SEAM
TO THE INSIDE AND HAND STITCH CLOSED. MARK
WHERE GROMMETS WILL BE PLACED.   CHOOSE A
LARGE HOLE PUNCH THAT WILL ACCOMMODATE
THIS SIZE GROMMET.   AS SUGGESTED BEFORE,
WORK ON A PIECE OF WOOD.

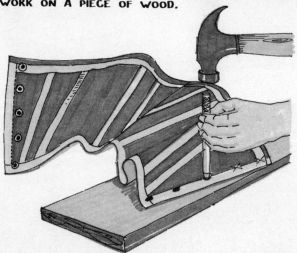

PUSH GROMMETS INTO HOLES
FROM FRONT SIDE OF FABRIC.
FLIP CORSELET OVER AND
POSITION SECOND PART OF
GROMMET INTO PLACE. USE
A HAMMER AND A SETTING
TOOL TO JOIN GROMMET
PIECES TOGETHER TIGHTLY
THROUGH FABRIC.

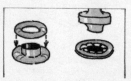

MAKE CORSELET STRAPS BY PINNING FABRIC AND
LINING TOGETHER. STITCH UP ONE SIDE AND
DOWN THE OTHER LEAVING THE BOTTOM OF
STRAP OPEN FOR TURNING. TURN AND PRESS.

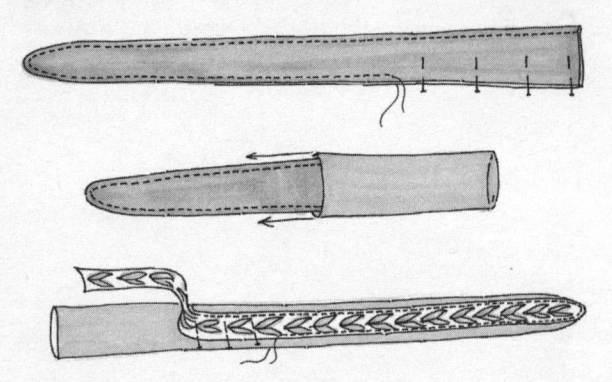

ADD TRIM. SERGE BOTTOM EDGE OF STRAP.
FIT CORSELET TO WEARER AND PIN STRAPS IN
PROPER POSITION. MACHINE STITCH STRAPS TO
CORSELET.

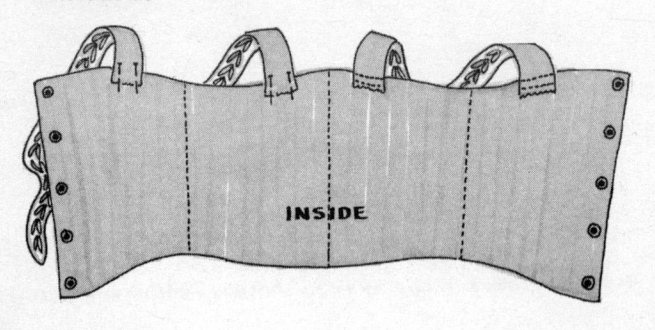

INSIDE

HERE ARE JUST A FEW OF THE DIFFERENT STYLES
THAT CAN BE ACHIEVED WITH THE ADDITION OF
TRIMS.

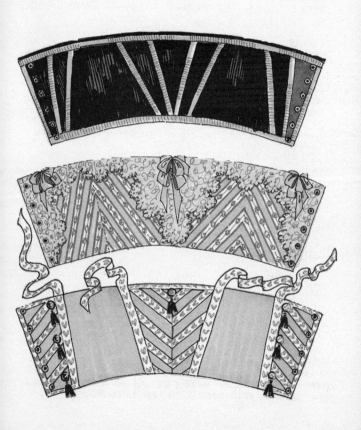

ENLARGE CORSELET AT BACK AND SIDE SEAMS.
THE ADDITION OF 1/4" TO THESE SEAM EDGES WILL
INCREASE THE PATTERN ONE SIZE.

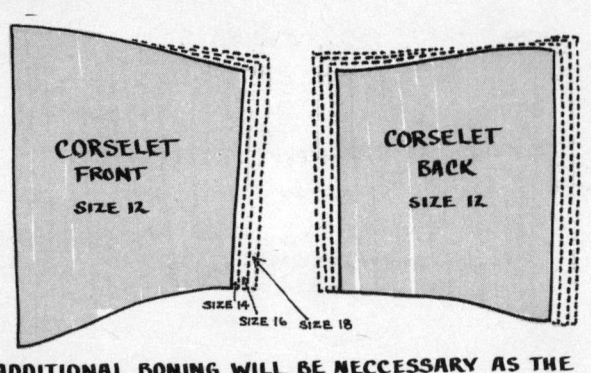

ADDITIONAL BONING WILL BE NECESSARY AS THE
CORSELET SIZE INCREASES.

FABRIC AND NOTIONS : 3/4 YD. FABRIC, 3/4 YD.
LINING FABRIC, 1/4 YD. IRON-ON CANVAS, 5
YDS. PLASTIC BONING, 8 YDS. TRIM, 10 SMALL
GROMMETS, HOLE PUNCH, GROMMET SETTER,
36" SHOE LACE OR LEATHER THONG.

FABRIC SUGGESTIONS : HEAVY WOVEN FABRICS
WITH A DESIGN, PETTIPOINT UPHOLSTERY
FABRIC, BROCADES, TRAPUNTO, CREWEL
WORK, SUEDE, VELVET.

TRIM SUGGESTIONS : METALLIC BRAID, LACE,
RIBBON, TASSELS, BUTTONS, APPLIQUES, BOLO
TIPS, FLOWERS.

SUPPLIERS: PERFORMING ARTS SUPPLY COMPANY
11437 TODD
HOUSTON, TEXAS 77055
1 [713] 681-8688

RICHARD THE THREAD
8320 MELROSE AVENUE
W. HOLLYWOOD, CALIFORNIA 90069
1 [213] 852-4997

AMAZON DRYGOODS
2218 E. 11 TH STREET
DAVENPORT, IA. 52803
1 [319] 322-4138

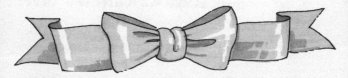

There is a romance and special
appeal about the corset. This
workbook endeavors to simplify
the interesting process of corset
building.

Bonnie Holt-Ambrose

SHOW #7...TRIMMING THE VICTORIAN WEDDING DRESS
       FROM SHOW 5.
SHOW #8...A SMALL BOY'S KNIGHT COSTUME THE
       EASY WAY.
SHOW #9...BUILDING LIGHT WEIGHT MEDIEVAL
       CROWNS.
SHOW #10..CONSTRUCTING AN INNVERNESS CAPE
       WITHOUT A PATTERN.

FOR A FREE BROCHURE AND FURTHER INFORMATION
CONTACT:
                BONNIE HOLT AMBROSE
                THE COSTUME WORKSHOP
                417 REINICKE
                HOUSTON, TEXAS 77007
                1 (713) 864-3969